I See the Tetons

Written and Photo-Illustrated by Erika Lincoln

Copyright © 2014 by Erika Lincoln
All rights reserved. This book or any portion thereof
may not be reproduced or used in any manner whatsoever
without the express written permission of the publisher
except for the use of brief quotations in a book review.
Printed in the United States of America
First Printing, 2014
ISBN 978-0-9913409-0-3

Dedicated to Paige, Kai and Beck. My wish for you is that you always see the beauty in life.

The rafter sees the Snake River.

The Snake River is 1,078 miles long. Every year many people flock to this river to fly fish, raft and kayak.

The person sees the Moulton Barn.

Part of a homestead complex built between 1912 and 1945 in Grand Teton National Park, Moulton Barn stands before the Teton Range.

The ranger sees the buffalo.

The buffalo is also known as the American Bison. A buffalo's weight can range from 700 to 2,200 lbs. Buffalo can run up to 35 miles per hour.

The cowboy sees the horse.

The horse is an icon of the American West. Many horses live throughout the Teton Range.

The moose is the largest species in the deer family.

Snowflakes are formed when water vapor freezes and falls from the sky. No two snowflakes are exactly the same.

The mountain climber sees Grand Teton.

Grand Teton is the highest peak in the Teton Mountain Range climbing to 13,775 feet (4,199 meters).

Elk live in or by the forest and eat bark, leaves, and grass.

The skier sees the tram.

The Aerial Tram travels to the summit of Rendezvous Mountain from Teton Village.

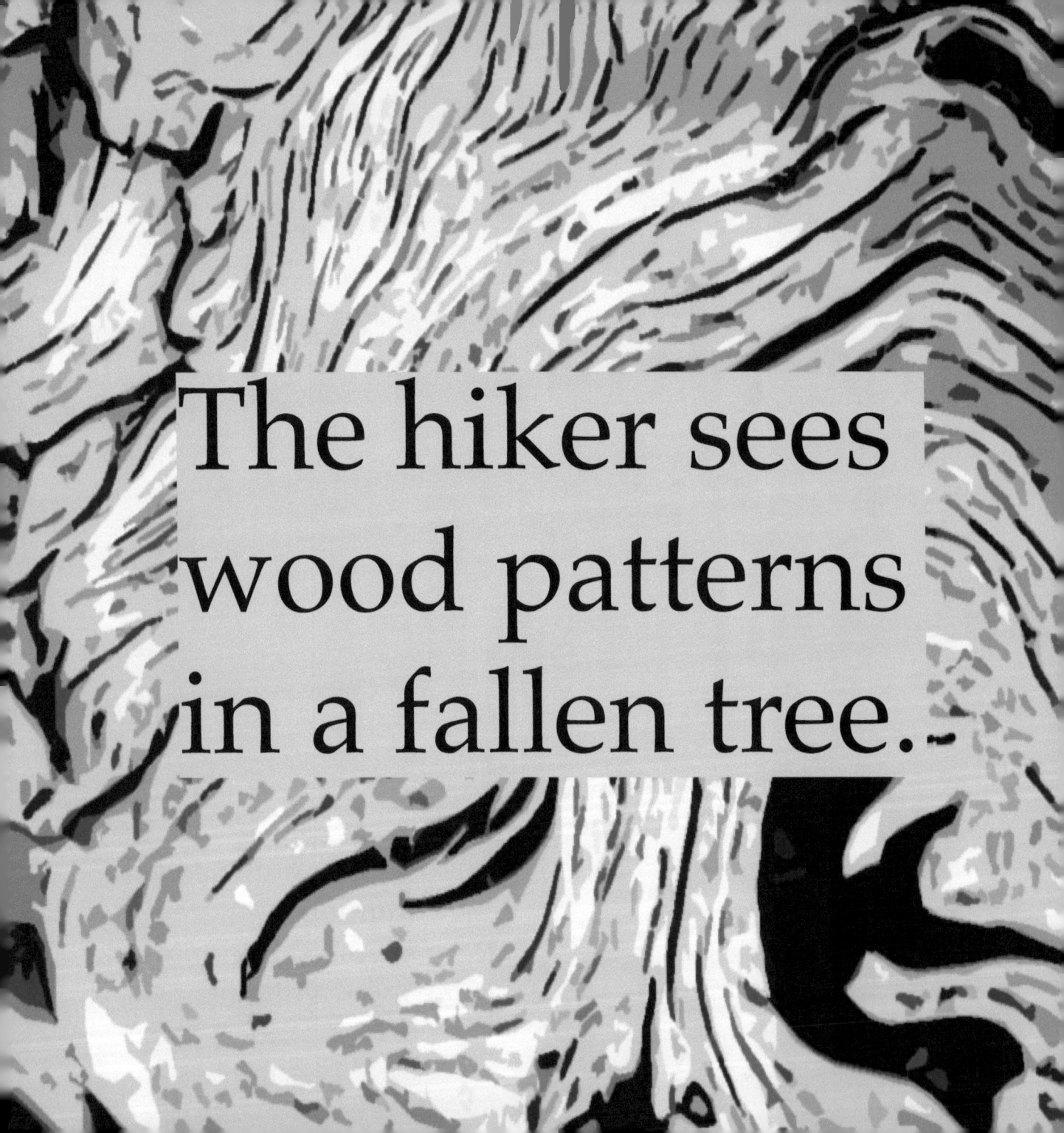

There are many types of trees in the Teton Range. Some are healthy and strong and some have fallen. All are part of a natural cycle of life.

The birdwatcher sees the Magpie.

The large magpie has a long black and white tail and a black bill.

The naturalist sees the conifer trees.

Conifer trees (also called evergreen trees) make up the majority of trees in Wyoming.

The family sees the arch of antlers.

Every year elk naturally shed their antlers. Elk antlers were collected to makes the arches in Jackson's Town Square.

The children see the beauty.

- Erika Lincoln

About the Author / Photo-Illustrator

Erika Lincoln is a poet and photographer. She is married to Andrew Lincoln and has three children - Paige and twin boys Kai and Beck. As a child, she started writing poetry and exploring the art of photography. At the age of 13, she published her first poem. She has transferred her childhood photography darkroom experience to modern digital photo illustrations seen throughout this book. Her love for the West and annual family visits to Teton County inspired this book.

-Enjoy

www.ingramcontent.com/pod-product-compliance
Lightning Source LLC
Chambersburg PA
CBHW042143290426
44110CB00002B/96